contents

W9-CFG-644

introduction

Welcome to the new London Transport Museum. Reopened in November 2007 after a £22m extension and refurbishment, the Museum tells the rich story of transport in London, from the first bus to the present day and into the future. Transport is what drives cities worldwide. As London grew to be a world city, its citizens moved from walking to using a complex mix of different transport modes: rail, taxi, bus, boat, tram, cycle.

The Museum collects and displays the legacy of two centuries of public transport in London. It is not just about the vehicles and equipment, but also the posters and artwork, timetables and tickets, photographs and memories. This guide summarizes the story told by the Museum galleries, weaving together a collage from our collections to demonstrate the central role of transport in the vitality and identity of one of the world's great cities.

Sam Mullins
Director, London Transport Museum

On the move around the globe: the Museum's first gallery compares urban transport in London with New York, Paris, Tokyo, Delhi and Shanghai.

moving **cities**

Transport is the lifeblood of cities.
Half the world's population now
lives in an urban environment.
Finding sustainable ways to keep
people on the move in our cities is
more important than ever before.

Historically, cities have developed
in distinct ways. Each has its own
character and complexity. But in
every case, transport and personal
mobility have played a key role in
city life past and present.

Transport will continue to be a vital
element in shaping our lives in the
future. With its huge and continuing
impact on the environment, it will be
a challenge for all of us, everywhere.

london – **the first world city**

VIEW OF LONDON
TAKEN FROM ALBION PLACE BLACKFRIARS BRIDGE

VUE DE LONDRES
PRISE D'ALBION PLACE PONT DE BLACKFRIARS

In 43AD, invading Roman armies crossed the Thames. They founded London, a port settlement that became a major centre for world trade. The city grew over time, but it was not until the late 18th century that the rapid growth began which created the urban giant of Victorian London.

In 1801, when the first census was taken, nearly one million people lived in London. By 1901, the year of Queen Victoria's death, the population had risen to 4.5 million in the London County Council area. Another two million lived in the growing ring of suburbs beyond.

London in 1800: an artist's view of St Paul's Cathedral and the City from the south side of Blackfriars Bridge. The bridge and River Thames are both crowded with goods and passenger traffic.

This huge metropolis with its government, business and residential districts, vast docklands, and industrial and commercial areas, was the greatest city the world had ever seen. Essential to London's success was the transport system that grew up and developed with the Capital in the 19th and 20th centuries.

By 2001 Greater London's population had reached 7.5 million, and it is still rising. London in the 21st century may no longer be the world's largest urban centre, but it is one of the most visited, diverse and cosmopolitan cities on earth.

London in 1900: the same view in an early colour postcard. Traffic is still horse-drawn over the road bridge, which was rebuilt in 1868. There is a steam tug on the Thames and a steam train on Blackfriars railway bridge beyond.

BLACKFRIARS BRIDGE & ST. PAULS' LONDON.

London in 2007: tower blocks encircle St Paul's on the City skyline. New electric commuter trains cross the river on Thameslink services. Buses have priority over cars in the Congestion Charge zone. There are wider pavements for walkers and designated cycle lanes. Riverboat services are reviving.

the **river**

The River Thames was vital to London's growth. International maritime trade had made London the busiest port in the world by 1800. The river was always crowded with ships of all sizes, mostly carrying cargo rather than people.

The first passenger transport along and across the river was provided by watermen using small rowing boats called wherries. These water taxis were the fastest way of getting around London, but watermen did have a reputation as hustlers. Unwary passengers could be taken for a ride in more ways than one.

Passenger traffic on the river increased rapidly after steamboats were introduced in 1815. The watermen gradually found themselves put out of business. By the 1850s Thames paddle steamers were carrying several million passengers a year. Many were pleasure-trippers, but every day at least 15,000 people travelled to work on the river.

The Thames was a barrier as well as a highway. In 1800 there were still only three bridges in central London. Fifteen new road and footbridges were built in the 19th century. Tower Bridge (1894) was the last and grandest of the Victorian river crossings.

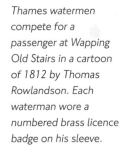

Thames watermen compete for a passenger at Wapping Old Stairs in a cartoon of 1812 by Thomas Rowlandson. Each waterman wore a numbered brass licence badge on his sleeve.

Tower Bridge was designed in the 1890s with the latest Victorian engineering technology, but it was made to look medieval. Underneath the decorative stone cladding was a steel structure and sophisticated lifting equipment which still functions today.

The Tower Bridge, London

THE TOWER BRIDGE.—APRIL-1892. B-1068

015

the **streets**

Two hundred years ago London was still quite compact. If you walked for half an hour in any direction from Westminster Bridge or St Paul's Cathedral, you would be out in the country.

For short journeys, everyone walked. The narrow streets of central London were often crowded with pedestrians, livestock and horse-drawn vehicles jostling for road space. Only the wealthy could afford to own a private carriage or ride around town in a hired hackney coach or sedan chair.

London's rapid expansion in the 19th century was almost completely unstructured. Streets did not follow the fixed grid used for American cities, nor the grand plans which reshaped European capitals like Paris and Vienna. A series of individual building schemes created a huge and sprawling metropolis with virtually no coordinated town planning.

London was the largest, richest city in the world, but poverty and overcrowding were never far away from the famous streets and impressive public buildings.

Life on the streets: Piccadilly Circus soon after completion in 1820 (top) and in 1900 after reconstruction (left). Crossing sweepers, including children, worked to keep the Victorian city streets clear of horse manure in return for a few pence from wealthier walkers (above).

cab and bus

Two new modes of transport came to the streets of early 19th-century London. Both were fashionable developments copied from Paris. The first was the cab, short for *cabriolet*. This was a light, two-wheeled vehicle which was easy to manoeuvre in the city. Horse-drawn cabs became a popular alternative to the heavy old

PADDINGTON
to the
BANK

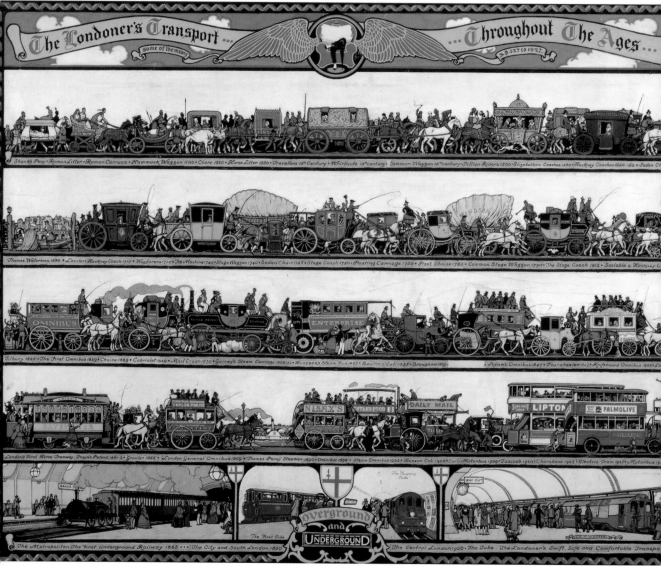

four-wheeled hackney carriages for hire on the streets. The design was gradually refined into the familiar Victorian hansom cab. The second innovation was the omnibus, meaning 'for all' in Latin. It was the name of a 'hail and ride' coach service started in Paris in 1828. English coachbuilder George Shillibeer (bottom right) brought the idea to London the following year.

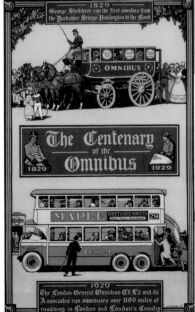

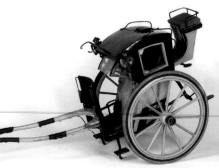

Coffin cab, c1835 (top right) and hansom cab, c1870 (above). A 1927 Underground poster (left) gives a colourful impression of Londoners' transport through the ages. Two years later the centenary of the London bus was celebrated and a working replica of Shillibeer's original vehicle was built, now on display in the Museum. Shillibeer's newspaper advertisement for his new service (right) appeared in 1829.

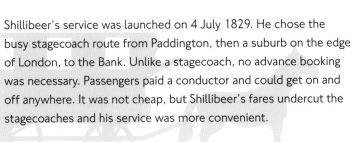

OMNIBUS.

G. SHILLIBEER, induced by the universal admiration the above Vehicles called forth at Paris, has commenced running one upon the Parisian mode, from PADDINGTON to the BANK.

The superiority of this Carriage over the ordinary Stage Coaches, for comfort and safety, must be obvious, all the Passengers being Inside, and the Fare charged from Paddington to the Bank being One Shilling, and from Islington to the Bank or Paddington, only Sixpence.

The Proprietor begs to add, that a person of great respectability attends his Vehicle as Conductor; and every possible attention will be paid to the accommodation of Ladies and Children.

Hours of Starting :—From Paddington Green to the Bank, at 9, 12, 3, 6, and 8 o'clock ; from the Bank to Paddington, at 10, 1, 4, 7, and 9 o'clock.

DERRING'S PATENT LIGHT SUMMER

Shillibeer's service was launched on 4 July 1829. He chose the busy stagecoach route from Paddington, then a suburb on the edge of London, to the Bank. Unlike a stagecoach, no advance booking was necessary. Passengers paid a conductor and could get on and off anywhere. It was not cheap, but Shillibeer's fares undercut the stagecoaches and his service was more convenient.

moving the crowds

Shillibeer's success prompted many imitators. Other operators began running omnibus services all over London. There were soon hundreds of horse-drawn buses on the streets, competing fiercely for passengers along the same routes. Conductors were paid by results and would dash ahead of their rivals in order to cram in as many passengers as possible. By the 1840s most London buses seated passengers not just inside, but outside on the roof, the earliest version of the double-decker.

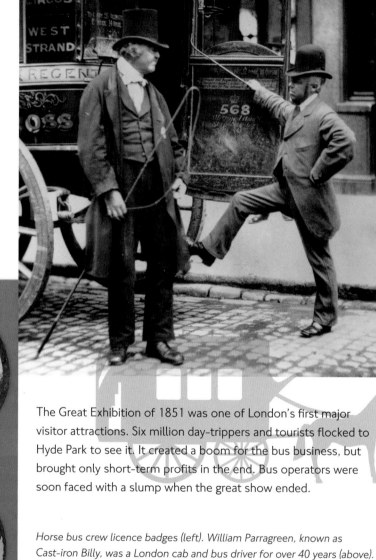

The Great Exhibition of 1851 was one of London's first major visitor attractions. Six million day-trippers and tourists flocked to Hyde Park to see it. It created a boom for the bus business, but brought only short-term profits in the end. Bus operators were soon faced with a slump when the great show ended.

Horse bus crew licence badges (left). William Parragreen, known as Cast-iron Billy, was a London cab and bus driver for over 40 years (above). The 1870s bus displayed in the Museum (far right) was operated by Thomas Tilling on the Times service between Oxford Street and Peckham.

The crisis was resolved by the creation of a single giant bus company in 1856. The London General Omnibus Company (LGOC) took over more than three quarters of the Capital's struggling operators in under a year. Only a few well-run family operations, such as Tilling and Birch, stayed independent. The LGOC suddenly became the largest bus company in the world. By the 1890s it was carrying well over 100 million passengers a year.

horse trams

Horse tram on the North Metropolitan Tramways system at Clapton, c1890. Horses were valuable assets and were better looked after than the staff. They worked shorter shifts than the drivers, with specially controlled diets and constant medical care.

The standard Victorian horse bus could carry about 26 passengers. A pair of horses could only manage to pull a larger and heavier vehicle if it ran on smooth iron rails in the road. Horse trams, as they were called, were first used on a street railway in New York as early as 1834.

It was an American, George Francis Train, who laid the first short tramway in London in 1861. He made the mistake of using protruding step rails which put other vehicles at risk. Train was forced to remove his tracks after only a few months' operation. Permanent street tramways were opened in London from 1870. By using vehicles twice the size of a bus, the tram companies could carry far more passengers and offer much lower fares. Few bus services ran before 08.00: well-timed for City clerks, but far too late for workmen. Early morning trams, on the other hand, gave thousands of working-class Londoners their first access to affordable public transport.

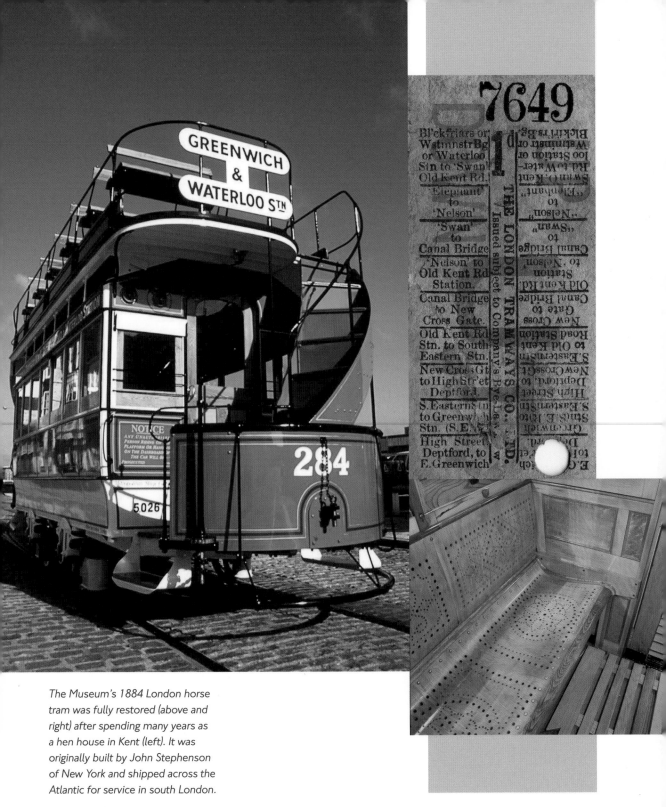

The Museum's 1884 London horse tram was fully restored (above and right) after spending many years as a hen house in Kent (left). It was originally built by John Stephenson of New York and shipped across the Atlantic for service in south London.

railways

Steam railways revolutionized transport in the 19th century. The first passenger line in London was the short London & Greenwich Railway, which opened in 1836. A year later, the first long-distance main line to the Capital, the London & Birmingham Railway, ran into Euston.

'It is very difficult nowadays to say where the suburbs of London come to an end and where the country begins. The railways, instead of enabling Londoners to live in the country, have turned the countryside into a city. London will soon assume the shape of a great starfish. The old town, extending from Poplar to Hammersmith, will be the nucleus and the various railway lines will be the projecting rays.'

Anthony Trollope, *The Three Clerks*, 1857

First-class commuters pose at Loughborough Junction (Brixton) station, c1890 (left), while working men and women arrive at Victoria on a third-class service in 1865 (right). Charing Cross (below left), one of London's new railway termini opened when lines from the south crossed the river into Westminster.

The railway boom of the 1830s and 1840s saw routes to London created from every direction. Most terminated some distance from the city centre, since Parliament was worried about demolition and disruption to the Capital. As a result, the railway companies originally had only limited permission to build their lines right into the City and Westminster.

However, the railways were a powerful force for change and kept expanding. Stations, yards and depots soon covered huge areas of land. In the process at least 100,000 Londoners,

mainly the poor, had their homes destroyed. The railway companies were forced to run cheap early-morning services into town as compensation. Few of those made homeless became daily commuters.

By the 1870s, nearly all people and goods moving in and out of

the growing metropolis travelled by train. In one way or another, the railways shaped every Londoner's daily life.

Sign board from the offices of the London & Blackwall Railway at Fenchurch Street station (below). This was the first railway terminus in the City of London, originally opened in 1841.

It seems incredible today that steam trains were used on the original London underground lines. To reduce pollution, exhaust steam from the cylinders was piped into a large side tank on the engine where it was condensed into cold water. The system was not very effective, as the photograph at Aldgate in 1902 suggests (top left).

world's first **underground**

By the 1850s, it could take longer to get across London by road than it took to travel to the Capital by train from Brighton, 80km (50 miles) away. The railways made it easier to get to London, but actually contributed to the growing congestion on the streets.

In 1860 work began on the first attempt to solve the problem: an underground railway. The Metropolitan Railway was designed to link three of London's main line termini with the City. It was built mostly in shallow cuttings excavated along the street, which were then roofed over. This method was known as cut-and-cover construction.

The first section of the Metropolitan opened from Paddington to Farringdon on 10 January 1863. A second underground line, the District, began operating five years later. The two were eventually linked to create the Circle line in 1884.

The early underground was a huge engineering achievement and very well used, but had one big disadvantage. Its steam locomotives created a permanent sulphurous fug in the stations and tunnels. The only surviving engine from the 1860s, Metropolitan number 23 (below), is on display in the Museum.

An army of 2000 navvies built the Metropolitan and District Railways in the 1860s. This view near Gloucester Road (above) shows the shallow cutting for the railway being covered over with cast-iron rings and a brick tunnel lining before the road surface is reinstated on top. Most of these robust structures are still in use today.

out to the **suburbs**

The railways made it possible for the Victorian middle classes to live some distance from their place of work. The original main lines were designed primarily for long-distance, inter-city travel, not daily commuting. More local lines and stations were opened after the 1860s, encouraging the growth of railway suburbs on the edge of London.

Surbiton was one of the earliest suburbs to be developed on open farmland around a railway station. Bedford Park,

The Museum's Metropolitan Railway coach (below) carried passengers to the growing suburbs and countryside northwest of London for over 60 years. Built in 1900, it was converted from steam to electric working, and finally used with steam engines again until 1960. The Southern Railway electrified the whole of its suburban network south of the river in the 1920s and 1930s (right).

SEPTEMBER 30TH 1935 AND UNTIL FURTHER

SOUTHERN RAILWA

2D

OFFICIAL

SUBURBA
TIME TABLE
CHEAP FARES AND
WEEKLY SEASON TICKET RATE

A steam train arrives at Bowes Park station around 1905 (above). This suburban service in north London did not get diesel trains until the 1960s. Golders Green had the convenience of a fast and clean electric Tube service from 1907 (right).

the first garden suburb of architect-designed homes, was conveniently situated close to the new District line station at Turnham Green in the 1880s.

Suburban development boomed all round London in the early 20th century where good local rail services were available. In an age before the private car, electric trams and motorbuses also made suburban living more appealing and convenient.

The record for speedy growth was probably set by Golders Green. In 1905 it was a country cross-roads. The Hampstead Tube arrived two years later. By 1913 Golders Green was a fully formed community with over 3000 homes and a shopping centre, cinema and theatre all just a few minutes' walk from the station. The West End was just a 20-minute Tube ride away.

UNDERGROUND

THE SOONEST REACHED AT ANY TIME

GOLDERS GREEN
(HENDON AND FINCHLEY)
A PLACE OF DELIGHTFUL PROSPECTS

METROPOLITAN LINE

LADIES ONLY

The 'Ladies Only' compartment of the Museum's Metropolitan Railway coach. Visitors can eavesdrop on the conversation of two fashionable women as they travel up to town from the suburbs of Metro-land for a day's shopping in the 1920s.

suburban lifestyle

Many Londoners got their first opportunity to buy their own home in the 1920s and 1930s. Developers were building new housing estates faster than ever before, especially in suburban districts served by the new Tube extensions and Southern Electric rail services. Building societies offered cheap mortgages, making it possible for many people to purchase rather than rent, which had been the norm in Victorian London.

A variety of changes in lifestyle came with a semi-detached house and a season ticket. One of the Museum's exhibits is a 1930s doll's house in the typical half-timbered style of

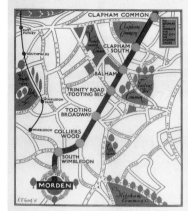

the period. These Tri-ang brand toys were mass-produced in suburban south London at the giant Lines Brothers works in Merton, opened in 1925. At the time, it was proudly promoted as the greatest toy factory in the world.

The Tube was extended from Clapham to Morden in 1926 (above). Feeder bus services connected the new Tube terminus with suburbs further out. The entire area around the station was soon covered in new semi-detached housing (below).

Most of London's inter-war suburban housing was traditional in design, like the Hounslow estate advertised here (left). The stylish modernist homes built conveniently close to the new Stanmore station in the 1930s (above) are interesting exceptions. Suburban life is captured in this 1930s doll's house (right), made in the Tri-ang toy factory.

This Underground poster by Fred Taylor appeared in 1925. It shows a gleaming new Tube station on the Edgware extension with house-building busily underway all around it. As transport extended out of central London, suburban development quickly followed.

metro-land

The Metropolitan Railway grew out of its original role as an underground link line in central London. By the 1890s its main extension line had been pushed overground through the north-west suburbs deep into London's countryside. The company chairman, Sir Edward Watkin, had grandiose plans to run the railway through to Manchester, and in the other direction to Paris through a proposed Channel Tunnel. He was a man ahead of his time.

Moving to Metro-land was promoted through posters, guidebooks and even on carriage door plates (left). The marketing campaign had a huge impact on the Metropolitan Railway's season ticket sales, which boomed in the 1920s. The last of the Met's own housing developments was the Weller Estate at Amersham, with purchase options shown in a colour brochure in 1930 (above right).

TYPE "B"

An exceptionally well planned 4 Bedroom Semi-Detached House with a built-in Garage. Constructed in brick with rough cast spar elevation and red tile roof, and having oak half timbering to the overhanging bay to first floor with red tiles under.

These properties have been erected in plots well set back from the Road in the corner of Woodside Close, conveniently situated within 3 minutes' walk of the Station and Shops, and facing a permanent open space.

This house could be repeated in The Drive, south of the Railway, on a plot with 33 feet frontage and a depth of about 130 feet at same price.

All the modern features are found in these houses. Tiled Bathroom, with enclosed bath, and Kitchen, leaded glass windows. Dwarf Brick Wall with posts and chains and chain link side fencing. Main Drainage.

£985 FREEHOLD

TOTAL DEPOSIT £25

NO ROAD CHARGES
NO STAMP DUTIES

METRO-LAND

BRITISH EMPIRE EXHIBITION NUMBER

PRICE. THREE-PENCE

Watkin's successors came up with a more practical and profitable scheme. The Met was the only railway to become a successful property developer, using surplus land alongside the line to build new housing estates. The whole area was marketed as Metro-land, a name first devised in 1915. Posters and a glossy annual guide were soon attracting new homebuyers out to Rayners Lane, Ruislip and Rickmansworth. By the 1930s much of Metro-land had become entirely suburban, but the outer areas still retain their rural character today.

Wembley Park was chosen as the site for the 1924 British Empire Exhibition. A huge national sports stadium was also built there. The twin towers of Wembley became Metro-land's most widely recognized feature.

Powerful new electric locomotives were introduced in 1922 to haul fast main line passenger trains from the City out to Metro-land. The Museum's locomotive number 5 'John Hampden', identical to the number 14 shown here, was used on these services until 1961.

heading out, **heading in**

London's transport services became almost as well used for evening and weekend leisure trips as for journeys to work. Very few Londoners owned a car, and the only way to visit the countryside in the early 20th century was by bike, train, tram or bus.

Rambling was very popular in the 1920s, and railway companies published guides to country walks for use with cheap excursion tickets. Sunday schools and social clubs organized bus and train trips to the country for inner-city and East End children.

The District line carries children to a day out in Eastcote, still rural in the 1920s. Walkers soon had greater access to the countryside around the Capital with the arrival of Green Line coach services in 1930. The stylish TF-type coach on display in the Museum (below) was London Transport's latest streamlined design in 1939.

GREEN LINE
LONDON TRANSPORT

Green Line coach services from London to country towns in the Home Counties started in 1930. The Green Line network grew after 1933 as part of London Transport's Country Bus division, which developed services all over London's country area.

The Underground became famous for its creative use of publicity posters. A changing display in the Museum demonstrates the astonishing range of graphic art styles used in the 1920s and 1930s to promote these off-peak services. The posters also show the variety that London could offer in the way of sport, leisure and entertainment.

Poster designs from the 1920s and 1930s encourage leisure travel by bus, coach and Underground out to London's countryside and in to the West End for evening entertainment.

Passengers use the
new escalators at
Holborn station, 1933.

Green Line services were introduced from central London to country towns all over the Home Counties in the 1930s. This coach is in Stevenage, Hertfordshire, passing a new London Transport bus shelter on the High Street in 1934.

Travelling by bus, tram or Underground to sporting events of all kinds was promoted in eye-catching publicity posters. Greyhound racing was a popular new spectator sport in London in the 1920s.

digging deeper

The shallow cut-and-cover construction method used for London's early underground lines was expensive and the work created chaos on the streets. Running a passenger railway in deeper tunnels under the city only became possible once three technological problems had been solved.

Engineers needed to perfect a safe and reliable tunnelling

ALL OUR OWN WORK

The world's most advanced underground railway, the Victoria Line, is now open, and London Transport would like to thank the men who built it: miners, like Black Jack's Gang above; engineers, architects and surveyors; planners, draughtsmen, electricians, steel erectors, carpenters, bricklayers, labourers. Their £70 million effort is now on permanent exhibition, and the price of admission is as little as five-pence.

London's pride

method, find an efficient mechanical means of moving passengers up and down at deep-level stations, and adopt a clean alternative to steam power for the trains.

Separate solutions to all three were brought together in London in the 1880s, making it possible to build the world's first deep-level electric Tube railway.

A specially designed cylindrical shield like a giant apple corer has been used to cut deep tunnels through the London clay for over a century. Lifts have made deep stations accessible since 1890, while escalators, which are better for moving large numbers of people quickly, were first installed in 1911 at Earl's Court station. By this time all underground lines were electric.

The dramatic low-level entrance hall for the Jubilee line station at Canary Wharf (left) was created in the 1990s by reusing a massive former London ship dock.

Deep-level tunnels in London are still excavated using a protective shield. The digging is now done by machine rather than by hand (far left) and the tunnel behind it is lined with cast iron or concrete rings to create a tube: hence the Underground's nickname.

pioneer tube

The City & South London Railway (C&SLR) opened in 1890. The first deep-level underground line was a triumph of innovative engineering, taking less than four years to complete. In contrast, Marc Brunel had devoted 18 years to building the much shorter Thames Tunnel from 1825-43, which was adapted to take the East London Railway in 1867.

Steam trains could never have been used on the C&SLR. The

original plan was to adopt the Hallidie cable-haulage system used for San Francisco's tramways and already running up Highgate Hill in north London. Halfway through construction, the radical decision was made to use electricity, never before applied to an underground railway.

The public opening of the world's first electric underground railway was delayed for six weeks after the royal inauguration in 1890. The line was well used in rush hours, but passengers did not like the windowless carriages. A gateman had to shout out each station name when the train stopped.

The electrical installation worked, but only just. There was barely enough power to run more than one train at a time, and the first electric Tube railway started operations with hydraulic lifts and gas lighting at every station.

The little C&SLR electric locomotive (right) and windowless 'padded cell' car (left) displayed in the Museum now look very primitive. But they represent the start of the electric Tube system which was the key to London's future transport.

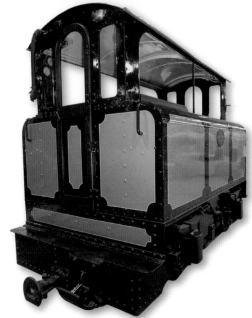

The original power station at Stockwell (above) soon had to be upgraded to provide enough electricity to run the trains.

Souvenir medallion (left) commemorating Brunel's Thames Tunnel, which opened in 1843 between Rotherhithe and Wapping.

electric underground

The success of the City & South London Railway led to a flurry of further deep-level Tube projects. But ten years after it opened, only two more had been completed. These were the short Waterloo & City line (1898) and the Central London Railway (1900).

The problem with the Tubes was not one of engineering, but the difficulty in financing the huge costs of construction. No government or local authority funding was proposed, and the likely financial returns on Tube schemes did not encourage private investors.

The Baker Street & Waterloo Railway named on this staff badge soon became known officially by its nickname: the Bakerloo.
The first free map, issued in 1908, was a joint production between the various private underground railway companies.

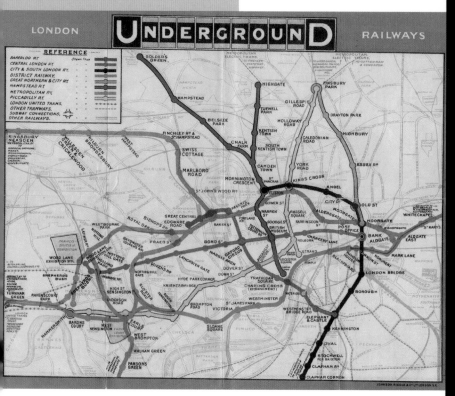

"THE MOVING SPIRIT OF LONDON."

THIS POWER-HOUSE BURNS 500 TONS OF COAL A DAY; IT CONTAINS—

8 TURBO-GENERATORS, running at
1000 REVOLUTIONS per MINUTE, developing
65,000 HORSE-POWER; to work
80 MILES OF RAILWAY
145 LIFTS and
900 CARS

For the USE and BENEFIT
of the PEOPLE OF LONDON

Control panels from Lots Road Power Station, Chelsea, (left). Charles Tyson Yerkes (below) began his bid to take over the London Underground by building this giant generating station to power all the lines. It was the biggest in Europe at the time.

The unlikely saviour of the London Underground was an American entrepreneur called Charles Tyson Yerkes. He had made a fortune running street railways in Chicago. Yerkes saw new opportunities in London and set up the Underground Electric Railways of London Company (UERL) in 1902.

The UERL took over and completed three struggling Tube projects, opening the Bakerloo, Piccadilly and Hampstead Tubes in 1906-7. Yerkes himself died in 1905, but his legacy to London was a high-quality Underground network, built very quickly and introducing the latest American electrical engineering systems.

creating
london transport

With the growing complexity of London's transport in the early 20th century, Londoners wanted better coordination of services. In practice this was difficult to achieve because of the conflicting interests of the various private and public transport operators involved.

The Underground Group had become the dominant operator by 1914. It expanded rapidly under the confident leadership of Albert Stanley, later Lord Ashfield. This giant private 'Combine', as it was often called, was responsible for most of the Underground, three tramway systems and London's main bus company, the London General Omnibus Company (LGOC). Outside the Combine were the Metropolitan Railway and the council-run tramways. There were also, by the 1920s, dozens of small 'pirate' bus companies competing on the streets with the LGOC.

London Transport's roundel device became an instantly recognized corporate symbol. It appeared on everything from Tube stations to trainee bus conductors' caps. Man Ray's modernist poster of 1938 (far right) even took it into outer space.

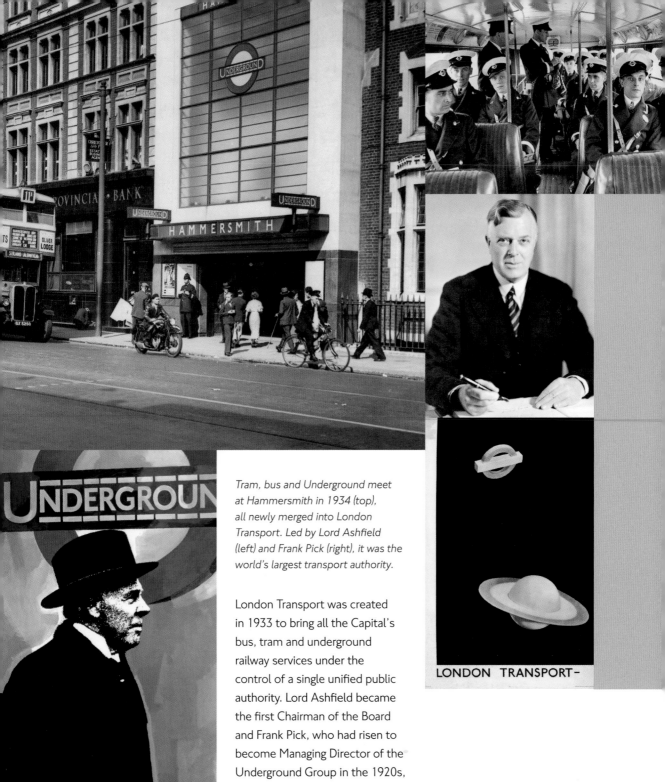

Tram, bus and Underground meet at Hammersmith in 1934 (top), all newly merged into London Transport. Led by Lord Ashfield (left) and Frank Pick (right), it was the world's largest transport authority.

London Transport was created in 1933 to bring all the Capital's bus, tram and underground railway services under the control of a single unified public authority. Lord Ashfield became the first Chairman of the Board and Frank Pick, who had risen to become Managing Director of the Underground Group in the 1920s, was made Chief Executive.

LONDON TRANSPORT-

transport **by design**

Frank Pick's energy and vision changed the face of public transport in London. He had a passionate commitment to good design and its importance at the heart of a well-run business.

For Pick, design was not an optional extra to make things look good, but a central part of 'fitness for purpose'. From vehicles and architecture to information and publicity, everything that was designed

for the Underground Group and London Transport contributed to the total effect. He wanted every element to show the organization as modern, efficient and confident.

Arnos Grove (left) and Southgate (above), two of architect Charles Holden's stations of 1932-33 on the Piccadilly line extension. Holden paid special attention to lighting design (below).

London Transport design: from bus stops by Hans Schleger, 1937, to Stockwell bus garage by Adie, Button and Partners, 1952. Iconic elements include tiling, Harry Beck's 1931 map design and the typeface, shown here on Edward Johnston's printing blocks, 1916.

The *Design for travel* gallery features a wide range of objects, models and images that show how London's main transport provider developed a distinctive house style and corporate identity through design. Edward Johnston's Underground lettering, the bar and circle symbol, Harry Beck's brilliant diagrammatic map of the Underground and Charles Holden's stylish station architecture were all part of this unique design culture.

The classic Underground look refined by Pick and Holden in the 1930s can be seen in Boston Manor station tower. This house style was reinterpreted in the 1990s when building Canada Water and the other Jubilee Line Extension stations (far right).

keeping it **fresh**

London Underground became a leading patron of modern art. Striking designs for publicity posters have been commissioned from both established artists and talented newcomers, turning Underground stations into London's biggest popular art gallery.

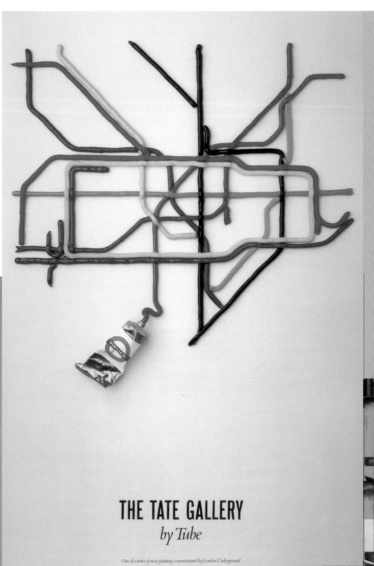

THE TATE GALLERY
by Tube

One of a series of new paintings commissioned by London Underground

A century of graphic design: posters by Abram Games (Zoo, 1976), David Booth (Tate gallery, 1986), Edward McKnight Kauffer (Winter sales, 1924), Tom Eckersley & Eric Lombers (By bus to the pictures, 1935) and Paula Cox (Dancing in the street, 1994). Lilian Dring's dramatic 1930s artwork (right) was never printed in poster form because it required a triple display site.

London Transport Museum holds a unique archive of more than 5000 posters and artworks covering a century of graphic design. They range from Frank Pick's earliest commissions to the latest works produced for Transport for London. As well as changing displays in the Museum, the whole collection can be viewed online at www.ltmuseum.co.uk.

underground **travel**

Travelling on the Underground has changed considerably over the last hundred years. The design of everything from train doors to ticket gates has developed and improved, but in some respects the experience of moving rapidly under London with a lot of other people you don't know remains much the same.

For the Edwardians, going by Tube was a new experience because it was classless. On the overground railways there had always been different classes of travel at different prices. The Tube was entirely democratic because everyone paid the same fare and travelled together.

The Lost Property Office at Baker Street (top) has had everything from umbrellas to funeral urns handed in over the years. The Museum's 1938 stock Tube car (far right) carried thousands of passengers in 40 years' service on the Northern line.

Overcrowding in rush hours has always been a problem. The American word 'straphanger' came into use a century ago to describe the passengers who couldn't get a seat and had to stand holding on to a leather strap.

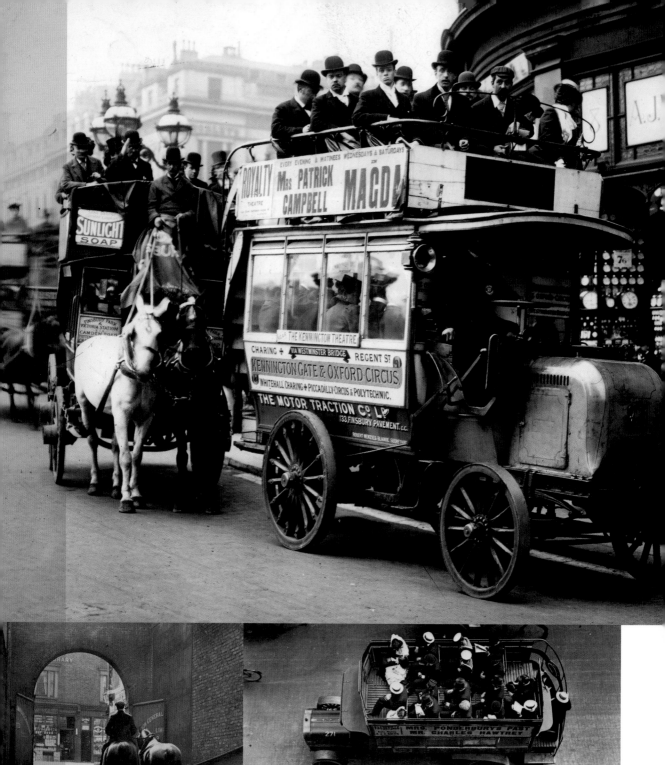

travel revolution

In 1900 virtually every vehicle on the streets of London was horse-powered. More than 300,000 horses were needed to keep the city on the move, hauling everything on wheels from private carriages and cabs to buses, trams and delivery vans.

While prototypes of mechanical vehicles were tested, most were unreliable and short-lived. Electric tramways had been introduced in a number of American and European cities in the 1890s, but London itself did not have a single line in operation at the turn of the century.

By 1915 everything had changed. There were no longer any horse buses or trams in London, and motor taxis heavily outnumbered horse-drawn cabs. Motorcars had replaced carriages, but only for the wealthy.

Motorbuses and electric trams were everywhere, and used by everyone. The effect on mobility in the city was enormous. The number of journeys Londoners made by bus and tram more than doubled. Horses had not yet disappeared from the streets. They were still used for most goods delivery, but in public transport the electric motor and petrol engine now provided all the power that London required.

A horse bus follows close behind London's first motorbus service, 1899 (above). This experimental vehicle with a Daimler petrol engine lasted only a few months. By 1907 more reliable motors were taking over (left) and soon horses were leaving the stables for the last time.

Mechanical transport for all: workers queue for early morning LCC electric trams in Catford, south-east London, in 1912 (left). A motor taxi outside the Savoy on the Strand offers a pricier personal service, c1907.

electric trams

Electric tramways opened all over Edwardian London in the early 1900s. There were soon 14 separate systems, 11 run by local councils and three by private companies. The first electric tram service in the Capital, running from Shepherds Bush into the western suburbs, was introduced by the private London United Tramways company in 1901.

Two years later the London County Council (LCC) opened its first electric route. This quickly grew into the world's biggest urban tramway system. Trams were kept out of the City and the West End, but were soon running along the Embankment and through a special tram subway built under Kingsway.

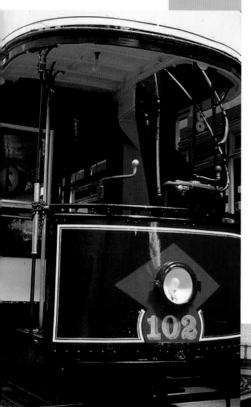

HIGHGATE ARCHWAY & ELECTRIC CAR

Workers construct the LCC Tramways electric conduit system on the Thames Embankment, 1906 (above). In outer London overhead wires were used for the power supply. Postcard views show Manor House (left) and Archway (below left). A West Ham Corporation tram of 1910 (far left) and a panel from the very first London electric tram of 1901 (below right) are on display in the Museum.

The LCC saw electric tramways as part of its social reform programme. Fast, cheap council trams would allow working-class Londoners to move out of the overcrowded city centre but still travel easily to work.

London's electric tram services were incredibly well used. By 1914, when trams were running down nearly every high street in London, they were carrying over 800 million passengers a year.

motorbuses

Finding a reliable mechanical alternative to the expensive horse for London's buses was not easy. Petrol engines looked more promising than battery electric or steam power, but none of the early experimental motorbuses coped well with London's demanding traffic conditions.

The breakthrough came with the famous B-type bus, designed in 1910 by Frank Searle, Chief Engineer of the London General Omnibus Company (LGOC). This was the bus equivalent of Henry Ford's Model T automobile. It was cheap, rugged and suitable for mass production. B-type engine units and chassis were soon being turned out at the rate of 20 a week from a factory in Walthamstow. Each one was fitted with a wooden body similar to the old horse buses. In under two years, the LGOC was able to replace its entire horse bus fleet with motors.

Many central London motorbus routes started in the early 1900s are almost the same today. By 1912 Sunday services ran out to the country. Motorbus drivers and conductors were issued with smart uniforms for the first time, and LGOC crews wore brass cap badges. On display in the Museum is B-type motorbus number 340, built in 1911 (below).

Motorbuses could run over much longer routes than horses. A route numbering system, which started in 1908 to replace the old horse bus route identification by colour, quickly evolved. The LGOC, still the largest bus company, decided on bright red as the standard colour for all its vehicles, the start of another London tradition.

first world war

The upheavals of the First World War (1914-18), which led to huge social change in Britain, are now almost beyond living memory. Fortunately, in the 1980s, the Museum was able to interview several former London transport workers about wartime transport. Although in their nineties, they vividly recalled their experiences of the Great War. These now feature in a special video programme in the *London's transport at war* gallery.

Florence Cordell became one of the first wartime 'conductorettes' in 1916. She describes her training on the buses, her reception in the all-male world of Willesden bus garage and the women's strike for equal pay. George Gwynn and Edward Darby both volunteered as drivers and took London buses to France (left), providing troop transport in the grim conditions of the Western Front.

DURING THE PRESENT CRISIS

PASSENGERS ARE RE-QUESTED TO KEEP THE BLINDS DRAWN at NIGHT

EAST OF BOW ROAD AND
WEST OF GLOUCESTER ROAD

ENGLAND v GERMANY.

SIGN ON AT ONCE FOR THE GRAND INTERNATIONAL FINAL.

EVERY MAN COUNTS.

Much to everyone's shock and surprise, London was bombed by German Zeppelin airships and later aeroplanes between 1915 and 1918, bringing the war to the civilian population. There was more disruption than damage, but 670 people were killed in the raids on London, including some bus and tram crews. A black-out was introduced and for the first time Tube stations were used as public air raid shelters.

A badge records battles on the Western Front where London buses served (top centre). Back in England, Florence Cordell became a wartime conductorette (middle left) and the Metropolitan Railway took on women guards (left). Staff follow the funeral cortège of Driver Tarrant and Conductor Rogers (above), killed when their bus was hit in one of the first air raids in 1915.

safety first

In 1901, when London traffic was still horse-drawn, there were 186 fatal road accidents in the city. In 1929, when motor vehicles dominated, 1362 people were killed on London's roads. Most private motorists had never been trained, and driving and safety standards were very poor.

Driving tests and a speed limit for urban areas of 30 miles per hour (48km) became compulsory in 1934. Traffic lights, pedestrian crossings and wide new arterial highways such as the Western Avenue and North Circular Road were introduced. Yet none of these innovations could solve the growing safety and congestion problems on London's streets.

Cycling became very popular between the two world wars. By the 1930s there were

MOTOR CYCLISTS. Do not squeeze through traffic, particularly on the near side. By reason of the inherent safety, speed and narrowness of their mounts, motor cyclists are inclined to take risks in squeezing through traffic (see picture). The temptation to pass on the near side of a car dawdling along the middle of the road is very great. It has, however, its dangers, for the car driver, suddenly brought to his senses by the noise of the motor cycle which he cannot see, may pull in to give the motor cyclist what he imagines to be more room ; or a traffic exigency may cause him to pull in and trap the motor cyclist. (No. 22.)

ON steep hills set the wheels against the kerb. If the car faces downhill, set front wheel against the kerb, as shown in illustration (blue car). If you are facing up lock your front wheels so that the back of near side front wheel is in contact with the (see illustration, red car). In both cases as the cars move, they would be brought to rest by the kerb. As an additional safeguard on steep hills engage bottom or reverse gear, for the engine forms a powerful brake. After scotching the wheels with stones, never leave the stones in the road, as they may cause an accident. (No. 23.)

CORRECTING a skid. Providing that the car is not travelling at excessive speed a skid need be an alarming occurrence. To correct a back wheel skid, close the throttle, avoid if possible applying the brakes, and turn the steering wheel in the direction in which the back of the car is skidding. To correct a front wheel skid, close throttle and momentarily apply the brakes. Assuming that brakes in perfect adjustment, and the tyres in good condition and correctly inflated, the main causes of skidding are bad driving, too sudden application of the brakes, or too rapid cornering. (No. 24.)

William Wagstaff rides his new Evans racing bike, 1929 (lower left). Road safety is taken seriously in a cigarette card album and poster (left), but not by a comic postcard of the period (below). Trafalgar Square, seen here with new traffic lights and crossing in 1934 (far left), was finally pedestrianized outside the National Gallery in 2003.

at least two million cyclists in the London area. One of the keenest was William Wagstaff, who had paid £13 for a brand new Evans racer in 1929 as a 20-year-old apprentice telephone engineer. When he married and moved out to suburban Croydon in 1938, he still commuted on 'Evans the bike' every working day and rode all over the country on touring holidays. His trusty cycle had covered thousands of miles under just one owner when his daughter presented it to the Museum in 2004.

trams overtaken

By the 1920s, London's buses were carrying more passengers than the trams. Covered top decks and pneumatic tyres improved journey comfort for passengers. Many more bus routes were introduced to serve London's new suburbs and country areas.

Trams were less flexible than buses because they were expensive to maintain and modernize. They started to lose money, and in 1931 a Royal Commission on Transport recommended that tramways should gradually be phased out. In London trams began to be replaced with trolleybuses that very year.

A trolleybus is basically a cross between a tram and a bus. It has an electric motor supplied with power from overhead wires,

London trolleybuses were big 70-seaters that could shift large crowds quickly and silently, as here in Tottenham after a Spurs home game in 1949 (top). But they could get easily dewired. The conductor then reconnected the trolley booms using a long bamboo pole (above).

but instead of running on fixed rails, it runs on rubber tyres and can be steered like a bus. Trolleybuses could use the same power distribution system as the trams, but were cheaper to run because there was no track to maintain. By 1940, when the conversion programme was interrupted by the Second World War, more than half of London's huge tram network had been replaced by trolleybuses. After the war, however, London Transport decided to standardize its road services with diesel buses. A completely new bus, the Routemaster (above), took over from the trolleybus fleet between 1959 and 1962.

second world war

When the Second World War (1939-45) broke out in September 1939, London Transport and the main line railways evacuated over 550,000 children, hospital patients and expectant mothers from the London area in just four days.

Women were again recruited to replace male staff who had joined the armed forces, but on a much larger scale than in the First World War. Many took factory jobs in London Transport's repair shops, which were turned over to war work, including aircraft construction. Over 700 Halifax bombers were completed by a workforce with almost no previous engineering experience.

AIR RAID
ALERT
HAS SOUNDED

GOOD BYE TRANSPORT   HITLEF

London was bombed every night for seven weeks, then intermittently until May 1941. In 1944-45 a final assault took place using flying bombs. More than 15,000 civilians were killed, including 426 London Transport staff, and thousands more were injured or made homeless.

When the Blitz began in September 1940, large crowds fled to the Tube for shelter from the bombs. This began unofficially, and with no proper facilities there were chaotic scenes at first. While providing an underground home every night for thousands of Londoners, the Tube was able to keep running throughout the war.

London at war (clockwise from left): Southern Railway staff helmet, children being evacuated by bus, air raid warning sign, bomb damage in Balham, recruiting poster for women conductors, shelter ticket for Covent Garden station, shelterers sleeping in the Tube and women lathe operators at Acton Works.

London Transport staff practise changing a rail at Neasden Depot wearing gas masks and protective clothing, March 1940. Fortunately, the threat of a gas attack never materialized.

GAS PUT ON YOUR MASK

The traffic grows, and the Londoner's dependence on his public transport grows, too ⊖ New circumstances need new techniques, new methods ⊖ New automatically-driven trains for the Victoria Line ⊖ New buses for London's Red Arrow and flat-fare routes ⊖ New machines for automatic fare collection to save staff on road and rail ⊖ More station car parks ⊖ London Transport must change to keep pace with the constantly changing pattern of London on the move ⊖

FESTIVAL OF BRITAIN

M. GAMES

TRANSPORT INFORMATION

in the ticket hall of CHARING CROSS (London Transport) STATION

These vehicles are carrying...

69 people who could all...

be on this one bus ➡

⊖

post-war london

After the Second World War, London's transport services were badly run down. But they were carrying more passengers than ever before. Most people still used public transport to get to the big events that brightened up the bomb-damaged city: the 1948 Olympic Games at Wembley, the 1951 Festival of Britain and the Queen's Coronation in 1953.

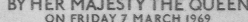
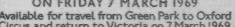

LONDON TRANSPORT SOUVENIR TICKET
OPENING OF THE
VICTORIA LINE
BY HER MAJESTY THE QUEEN
ON FRIDAY 7 MARCH 1969
Available for travel from Green Park to Oxford Circus and return to Victoria on 7 March 1969

In the 1950s, many Londoners got their first television set. With entertainment at home, they were less likely to take the bus to the cinema or a football match. Bus travel went into decline, although in London's country area, the growth of New Towns such as Stevenage, Harlow and Crawley boosted use of Green Line and country buses.

Between 1950 and 1975 the number of private cars in London grew from 480,000 to nearly three million. Traffic congestion got worse, and the reliability of bus services went down. London Transport found it had too many buses and not enough passengers.

The biggest transport project in post-war London was the Victoria line, the first new Tube under central London in 60 years. When the Queen opened it in 1969, it was the most advanced underground railway in the world, with fully automated trains and ticketing.

Congestion on the Finchley Road in 1959 (left) sums up London Transport's biggest post-war problem. After the success of the 1951 Festival of Britain, 1960s posters suggest that congestion was beyond LT's control. While the new Victoria line was a cause for celebration, limited funding for the Jubilee line that followed in 1979 delayed the project's completion for another 20 years.

working for **london transport**

London Transport at its peak in 1950 had nearly 100,000 staff. It was the biggest employer in London, moving millions of people through the city every day. Most passengers saw only the uniformed staff who sold them tickets and operated the buses and trains. But behind the scenes were thousands more who planned, developed, supported and maintained the world's largest urban public transport system. Free travel, subsidized catering and a wide range of social and sports

facilities were all promoted to encourage more recruits. However, relatively low wages and unsocial shift work made transport jobs less attractive. Using direct recruitment from the Caribbean and special campaigns to attract women, London Transport increasingly reflected the growing diversity of the city's population.

From the 1950s London bus conductors used the ingenious Gibson roll ticket machine (left), designed by a member of staff. Jill Viner (above) became London's first woman bus driver in 1974. All London Transport staff could use the sports and social clubs (far left). Every day a vast catering operation supplied canteens all over London from LT's Food Production Centre at Croydon (middle left).

london icons

The black cab and red double deck bus are iconic symbols of London. They are recognized across the world. The classic 1950s versions of both became London standards and were still on the streets of the Capital at the start of the 21st century.

The FX4 cab launched in 1958 was in production for 40 years. A successor was finally unveiled in 1997. The TX1 had a fashionably 'retro' appearance combined with all the latest access and performance standards required for licensed cabs in London. Visitors to London Transport Museum can explore the latest TX4 version of the cab and test themselves against the legendary 'Knowledge' of London that all cabbies have to learn before getting a licence.

The Routemaster bus, which entered service in 1959, is the only one that many Londoners know by name. It represents a peak of the high-quality

FX4 cabs and a Routemaster bus at the symbolic heart of the city, Piccadilly Circus, 1965 (below left). The Routemaster was the last bus designed and built specially for London. The current TX4 cab is an updated version of the classic London black cab now appearing in other cities (top right).

vehicle design partnership developed over decades between London Transport and AEC, the company in west London that built most of the Capital's buses until the 1970s.

The last Routemaster retired from regular London service in 2005, but two heritage routes now run close to the Museum along the Strand.

Some Routemasters were in service for 40 years, but could not be adapted to meet modern access requirements. London Transport Museum has preserved five, including the prototype RM1. Routemasters still run on heritage routes 9 and 15.

overground **rail**

In 1948 the four main line railway companies were nationalized along with London Transport. Unfortunately London's rail infrastructure was not a priority for government investment in the years of post-war austerity. Electrification and modernization of overground services were slow compared to the pre-war years when the Southern Electric suburban network had been created south of the river. Ageing steam trains continued to provide many of the services in north London until the 1960s.

Waterloo, London's largest station, in 1947 (left); one of the last steam trains leaving Marylebone, 1966 (top left); Heathrow Express service at Paddington, started 1998 (below); the first Eurostar train at St Pancras International, 2007 (above).

By the 1980s improvements to the main line railways made it possible to commute to London from all over south-east England. Passenger services across London were opened up with the north-south Thameslink connection. Electric trains soon linked central London with Heathrow, Gatwick, Luton and Stansted airports.

When the Channel Tunnel opened in 1994, the Victorian dream of direct rail services from London to Paris and Brussels was realized. The new high-speed main line running under the city to the dramatically refurbished St Pancras station from November 2007 signals the start of a new railway age for 21st-century London.

light **rail**

Since the 1980s many cities in Europe and North America have rediscovered the benefits of trams, now often called 'light rail', as a mode of urban transport. They are much cheaper to install than 'heavy' suburban railways or metros. Environmentally they are better and more attractive to users than conventional diesel buses.

The first London scheme was the fully automated Docklands Light Railway (DLR), opened in 1987. The DLR has been a key feature in regenerating the city's run-down former docks area as a new business and residential district, centred on Canary Wharf in the Isle of Dogs. The DLR has been continually improved and extended, becoming the fastest-growing and most reliable railway in the country.

The Docklands Light Railway has been growing for 20 years and will expand further to serve the 2012 Olympic sites around Stratford and the Thames Gateway. City Airport station (far right) opened in 2006. Tramlink has brought fast modern trams to south London, improving access to Croydon's office and shopping centres.

The DLR runs mainly above ground level on elevated tracks. London's second light rail project, opened in 2000, was Croydon Tramlink. This is a more conventional tram scheme, and mixes street running with use of existing suburban railways. Tramlink has successfully attracted many local car users in south London back on to public transport. Cross-River Tram, a north-south light rail route crossing central London, is currently at the consultation and planning stage.

your **tube**

London Underground carries more than three million passengers a day. The numbers are rising, and in 2006/7 one billion passenger journeys were recorded in a 12-month period for the first time ever.

Providing a safe and comfortable travelling environment for so many people is an enormous challenge to those who are responsible for planning and operating the network. Everybody wants to get to their destination as quickly and efficiently as possible, but using the Tube can be a daunting experience, especially for those who are new to it.

Understanding the Underground is an interactive space where Museum visitors can find out more about how the Tube works and the best way to use it. Visitors can drive a train, explore the map, help other customers and check out the safety systems.

transport for london

Transport for London (TfL) was created in 2000 as a new integrated authority to replace London Transport, but with much wider responsibilities. TfL is chaired by the Mayor of London and implements his transport strategy through running London Buses, London Underground, Docklands Light Railway, London Rail, London River Services, Croydon Tramlink, Victoria Coach Station, Public Carriage Office (governing taxis and private hire vehicles), Street Management and London Transport Museum.

TfL inherited a transport system suffering from decades of underinvestment. Since its inception in 2000, Londoners have seen substantial investment and considerable improvement. London's buses have been modernized and made environmentally friendly, fully accessible and more frequent. Bus use has increased by 40% in the Capital, reversing a long-term decline.

There has been a switch from private car usage to public transport of nearly 5%, the first ever shift of its kind in a world city. Congestion charging has led to a significant reduction in city centre traffic, while the Oyster smartcard ticketing system and online Journey Planner have made travel simpler. Underground stations and trains are being refurbished, while TfL support has increased the use of river services, improved road safety and encouraged a 50% increase in cycling.

Stratford is set to become London's busiest new transport hub. The Stratford Central complex already has convenient interchange between overground rail, two Underground lines, the Docklands Light Railway and local buses. It will soon be linked to continental Europe via the nearby Stratford International station and the new High Speed One main line services from St Pancras to Kent and the Channel Tunnel.

visionary **london**

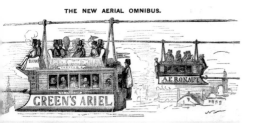

The last two centuries have seen many highly creative ideas about how London's transport might work in the future. They have ranged from satirical fantasy to science fiction, from the almost practical to the wildly unrealistic.

When the future arrives, it often turns out to be less fantastical than the visionaries predicted. Some big ideas, however, do eventually become reality.

Past futures (clockwise from above): London 2026AD, Underground poster, 1926; Dan Dare and the Red Moon Mystery, Eagle, 1952; George Bennie Railplane, Modern Wonder magazine, 1937; London Central Airport Hub Plan, 1930; and Punch's New Aerial Omnibus, 1847.

EAGLE-BRITAIN'S NATIONAL STRIP CARTOON WEEKLY

FOURPENCE-HALFPENNY

EVERY FRIDAY

EAGLE

25 APRIL 1952 Vol. 3 No. 3

DAN DARE
THE RED MOON MYSTERY

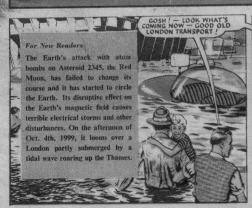

For New Readers

The Earth's attack with atom bombs on Asteroid 2345, the Red Moon, has failed to change its course and it has started to circle the Earth. Its disruptive effect on the Earth's magnetic field causes terrible electrical storms and other disturbances. On the afternoon of Oct. 4th, 1999, it looms over a London partly submerged by a tidal wave roaring up the Thames.

GOSH! — LOOK WHAT'S COMING NOW — GOOD OLD LONDON TRANSPORT!

I WON'T ARGUE ABOUT THE FARE THIS TRIP.

LONDON TRANSPORT

AND SIMULTANEOUSLY THE REST OF THE WORLD REELS UNDER THE BLOWS OF THE FIRST ORBIT OF THE MYSTERIOUS RED GLOBE.

NEW YORK CALLING EMERGENCY CONTROL. THE LAST TREMOR SURE SHOOK THINGS UP! MANHATTAN ISN'T AN ISLAND ANY MORE — THE EAST RIVER'S DRY AS A BONE...

ALLEZ! VITE! LÀ — TREMBLE- MENT DE TERRE!

PAS DE CALAIS

CROIX + ROUGE

AMBULANCE

LOVETOWN FIRE DEPT.

coming soon to **london**

London is set to grow and prosper in the future, with over 800,000 extra people and over 900,000 extra jobs forecast by 2025. This means a projected increase of four million journeys in the city every day.

The challenge is to improve London's public transport system to accommodate this growth, but at the same time manage overcrowding, reduce traffic congestion and cut carbon dioxide (CO_2) emissions.

A Low Emission Zone for London is introduced in 2008. Other planned transport developments include the Thames Gateway bridge (below), new DLR trains and stations (centre) and overground station redevelopment at Blackfriars and London Bridge by Network Rail (far right).

A wide variety of improvements to public transport infrastructure and services in London will take place in the near future. Proposals range across the Capital from new bridges and trams to overground rail links and the Crossrail project. Integrating these services effectively and considering their impact on the carbon footprint of the city will be of paramount importance.

The Low Emission Zone.
Cleaner air for Greater London.

Low emission ZONE

MAYOR OF LONDON

From 4 February 2008, if you drive a lorry, bus or coach you could be affected.
Visit tfl.gov.uk/lezlondon or call 0845 607 0009

Transport for London

A computer-generated image shows, from the north bank of the Thames, Network Rail's planned new Thameslink overground rail station on Blackfriars Bridge.

098

green futures

Climate change is the biggest single challenge facing London today. Its effects will be a major factor in determining London's future and the quality of life for its population. All of us as individuals, companies and global citizens have a role to play in tackling climate change and enhancing the environment.

London 2055 is an interactive space in the Museum which allows visitors to explore different scenarios for London's future, according to how they manage their carbon footprint. The rate of future climate change depends on the individual and collective choices and decisions we make today.

The green red bus: powered by hydrogen fuel cells, these buses only emit water vapour. They have been successfully trialled in London, and there are more to come.

covent garden flower market

The stunning building that houses London Transport Museum was once a Victorian flower market. Selling 'fruits, flowers, roots and herbs', markets were established in Covent Garden by the Earl of Bedford in 1670. By the 19th century, Covent Garden had become London's principal vegetable, fruit and flower market. In the 1830s permanent buildings replaced the traders' stalls in the central square. As the market expanded, additional buildings for specialist trading grew up around the piazza.

The Museum's building was designed as the dedicated Flower Market by William Rogers in 1871. For the next hundred years, this was the heart of London's wholesale flower business, famously trading every day except Christmas.

In 1974 all the market businesses moved out to modern warehouses at Nine Elms in south London. The old market buildings in Covent Garden were restored and the Flower Market reopened as the home of London Transport Museum in March 1980.

Covent Garden's heritage (clockwise from above): the Flower Market's restored clock; a 1908 sign on the station platform; Flower Market glass and ironwork; Underground poster by John Griffiths,1965; interior of the Flower Market, 1974; postcard of the central market building, c1905; flower girls,1877.

BARB AND ROSES, sweet peas and prima donnas, mingle in ~~glorio~~us confusion at Covent Garden. At six in the morning this great ~~marke~~t is a dazzling sight. In the quiet of evening, fashionable shoes pick ~~their~~ way through vegetable remnants towards Bellini, Verdi or Mozart. ~~At th~~e western end stands St. Paul's Church, Inigo Jones's 'handsomest ~~barn i~~n England'; pillared, imposing, and confusingly back-to-front.

Underground to Covent Garden ⊖

The cast-iron and glass architecture has an appropriate feel for a transport museum, being similar to a Victorian railway station. A major redesign in 2005-7 has respected the listed historic structure, but included improvements to stabilize the environment and incorporate energy-saving features such as photovoltaic cells on the roof to provide electrical power.

Covent Garden Market.

find out **more**

London Transport Museum
39 Wellington Street
Covent Garden
London WC2E 7BB

Call +44 (0)20 7565 7299
for opening hours, travel
and other information

www.ltmuseum.co.uk

Shop till you drop
What was once an entrance
into Covent Garden's Victorian
flower market is now our stylish
contemporary shop selling
souvenirs, designer gifts, books,
toys, limited edition models
and furniture. Among the shop's
most popular items are iconic
posters spanning a century of
transport design, including art
deco classics of the 1930s.
You can also shop online at
www.ltmuseum.co.uk.

Take the heat off your feet
The café and bar overlook
Covent Garden piazza and the
Museum's *World Cities* gallery.
During the day, enjoy morning
coffee, lunch and afternoon
tea. In the evening the space
transforms into a relaxing bar
providing a unique setting for
a London evening out.

Explore more
In the Learning Lounge above
the CBS Outdoor Gallery, relax
and delve more deeply into the
fascinating, often surprising
stories told in the Museum.
Visitors can watch films,
explore thousands of posters
and photographs online, or
browse through a selection
of publications.

The Library's specialist
collection of over 12,000 books
and pamphlets is available to
visitors Monday to Friday
by appointment. Explore
the extraordinary history of
London's transport, from its

architecture and design to the role it has played in the lives of Londoners over the past 200 years.

Pick up an events calendar or look online to enjoy exhibitions, films, tours, talks, children's activities, family fun days and off-site events around London.

Sign up for our regular e-newsletter and keep up to date with special events and activities. These include behind-the-scenes tours of the collections and open days at the Museum Depot in Acton, west London. Over 375,000 items are kept here, from buses and trains to artworks, posters and photographs.

find out **more**

Visit our virtual museum

At www.ltmuseum.co.uk explore transport through urban design icons, suburbia, war, Victorian London or transport futures.

Every picture tells a story

The Museum's image collection covers 150 years of history. More than 15,000 photographs and film clips can be viewed online at www.ltm.collections.org. Specialist researchers can make an appointment to view the reserve collections at the Museum Depot in Acton.

Schools

London Transport Museum learning programmes use the collection and its stories to support work in schools while providing inspiration to bring the history of transport to life. Flexible learning packages include on-site sessions with actors, quizzes, trails around the galleries and classroom investigations.

We also offer outreach sessions to secondary schools, in which pupils can study objects from the Museum, carry out investigations and debate past, present and future transport schemes.

The Safety & Citizenship team work mainly with young people aged 10 to 11 to prepare them for independent travel before they move to secondary school. The aim of this initiative is to promote safety and good citizenship on and around London's transport system. Using multimedia presentations and role play, the interactive sessions focus on how to make safe journeys with confidence and respect fellow passengers.

Lifelong learning

The Museum also works closely with the further and higher education sector. We offer group visits, courses, presentations and seminars on a range of topics from art and design in the urban environment to transport planning and engineering.

Hold a special event

Book London Transport Museum
to hire one of London's most
distinctive venues. The gallery
spaces can accommodate large
receptions or intimate dinners,
and provide an unusual backdrop
for business gatherings, product
launches, award ceremonies and
private celebrations.

Guests can mingle alongside
one of the world's most famous
icons – the red London bus – or
enjoy the modern displays that
mix the old and new in galleries
that focus on transport futures,
world cities, art and design and
Metro-land. The Museum can
accommodate 500 guests at
a cocktail reception and 200
people for dinner.

The Cubic Theatre seats 120
people, with state-of-the-art
presentation technology
and adjoining facilities for
meetings and entertaining.
It is fully accessible and can
be hired separately from the
main Museum.

london transport museum **friends**

London Transport Museum Friends is a registered independent charity overseen by a Board of Trustees. The organization has over 1500 individual members who are all committed to supporting the activities of London Transport Museum and the care and development of its collections.

The Friends raised £700,000 towards the Museum redevelopment. Their fundraising activity has also financed numerous conservation and restoration projects, including the Museum's unique 1931 LT-type 'Scooter'

single deck bus. With careful research work and specialist restoration skills, the Scooter was transformed from a rusting wreck to a gleaming London Transport bus, just as it would have been turned out from Chiswick Works more than 70 years ago.

The Friends organize meetings, visits and other special events, and publish a regular newsletter. There are wide-ranging opportunities to get involved in activities which assist the Museum's work, including guiding, cataloguing and recording oral histories.

Individual Friends contribute many hours of valuable volunteer work to the Museum each year.

Membership benefits include free admission to the Museum at Covent Garden during normal opening hours, advance information and concessionary booking for Museum events, and discounts on purchases in the shop.

Anyone can become a London Transport Museum Friend. For membership details pick up a form, write to the Museum or email friends@ltmuseum.co.uk

picture **credits**

Bridgeman Art Library p17, top; Creator Communications p100; Dan Dare Corporation p95; Docklands Light Railway p87, bottom right; p97, centre; Getty Images pp6-7; p58, bottom right; p73, shelterers; Dennis Gilbert p53; Guildhall

Library p12; Illustrated London News p94, proposed airport; IPC Media p94, Modern Wonder; LCR/TROIKA p85, top; LTI Vehicles p81, top right; Network Rail p97, right; p98; Tim Soar p43, main image; p92.

Helping to preserve London's transport heritage: the Friends have enabled the Museum to transform a 1931 London Transport bus from a wreck (centre) to a prize winner (right). The Friends' current major project is to restore a historic District line Q-stock Underground train (left) as a working heritage unit.